FAVORITE BASEBALL ★ TEAMS ★

ATLANTA BRAVES

BY K. C. KELLEY

The Child's World

Published by The Child's World®
1980 Lookout Drive • Mankato, MN 56003-1705
800-599-READ • www.childsworld.com

ACKNOWLEDGMENTS
The Child's World®: Mary Berendes,
    Publishing Director
The Design Lab: Kathleen Petelinsek, Design
Shoreline Publishing Group, LLC: James
    Buckley Jr., Production Director

PHOTOS
Cover: Focus on Baseball
Interior: All photos by Focus on Baseball except:
AP/Wide World: 10, 17, 18, 22 (2), 23, 25 bottom, 26.

LIBRARY OF CONGRESS
CATALOGING-IN-PUBLICATION DATA
Kelley, K. C.
  Atlanta Braves / by K.C. Kelley.
    p. cm. — (Favorite baseball teams)
  Includes index.
  ISBN 978-1-60253-375-2 (library bound : alk. paper)
  1. Atlanta Braves (Baseball team)—History—Juve-
nile literature. I. Title. II. Series.
  GV875.A8K45 2010
  796.357'6409758231—dc22   2009039444

Printed in the United States of America
Mankato, Minnesota
November 2009
F11460

On the cover: Derek Lowe, Pitcher

CONTENTS

Go, Braves!

Fans all over the South cheer for the Atlanta Braves. Thanks to cable TV, the team has fans from coast to coast, too! Many great players have played for the Braves over the years. The team has had many successful seasons. Millions of fans are looking forward to more big wins in the future! Let's meet the Braves.

High five (and a fist bump) as the Braves celebrate another win. ▸

Who Are the Braves?

The Atlanta Braves are a team in baseball's National League (N.L.). The N.L. joins with the American League to form Major League Baseball. The Braves play in the East Division of the N.L. The division winners get to play in the league playoffs. The playoff winners from the two leagues face off in the **World Series**. The Braves have won three World Series championships.

◀ One out, two more to go . . . great Braves action against the Reds.

Where They Came From

The Atlanta Braves are one of the oldest teams in baseball. They have not always played in Atlanta, however. The team was in Boston from 1876 through 1952. While in Boston, they were called the Braves, the Bees, the Rustlers, and the Beaneaters! They played as the Milwaukee Braves from 1953 through 1965. In 1966, the team moved to Atlanta. They have played there ever since. The Braves have won at least one World Series in each of their three homes!

Outfielder Jordan Schaefer is one of the young Braves players who will ▶ try to carry on a winning tradition.

Who They Play

The Atlanta Braves play 162 games each season. That includes about 16 games against the other teams in their division, the N.L. East. The other East teams are the Florida Marlins, the New York Mets, the Philadelphia Phillies, and the Washington Nationals. Atlanta's games against the tough Phillies teams are always exciting! The Braves also play some teams from the American League. Their A.L. **opponents** change every year.

◀ The Braves score another run in an action-packed game against the Phillies.

11

Where They Play

Turner Field is the home of the Atlanta Braves. The first sport in the stadium wasn't baseball, however. It was track! The stadium was the site of the 1996 Summer Olympics. After the Olympics were over, the stadium became a baseball ballpark. It was named for Ted Turner, a businessman who once owned the team. Turner Field holds more than 50,000 baseball fans.

A statue of old-time Braves ballplayers stands outside Turner Field. ▶

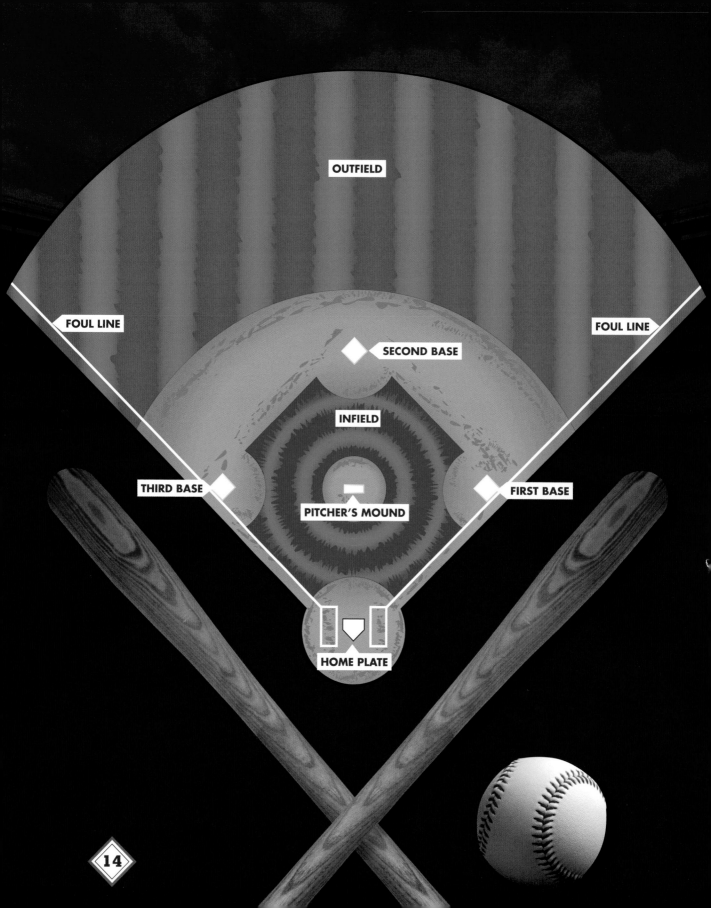

OUTFIELD

FOUL LINE

FOUL LINE

SECOND BASE

INFIELD

THIRD BASE

FIRST BASE

PITCHER'S MOUND

HOME PLATE

The Baseball Diamond

Baseball games are played on a diamond. Four bases form this diamond shape. The bases are 90 feet (27 m) apart. The area around the bases is called the **infield**. At the center of the infield is the pitcher's mound. The grass area beyond the bases is called the **outfield**. White lines start at **home plate** and go toward the outfield. These are the foul lines. Baseballs hit outside these lines are out of play. The outfield walls are about 300-450 feet (91-137 m) from home plate.

Big Days!

The Braves have had many great seasons in their long history. Here are three of the greatest:

1914: In late July, the Boston Braves were in last place. They were 14 games behind first place. Then they became the "Miracle Braves." The team came back to win the N.L. In the World Series, they upset the powerful Philadelphia A's!

1957: The New York Yankees had won six of eight World Series. But this year, they were up against a great Milwaukee Braves team. Three big wins by pitcher Lew Burdette helped the Braves win their second World Series.

1995: Pitcher Greg Maddux won 19 games. **Sluggers** Fred McGriff, Ryan Klesko, and Chipper Jones smacked homers. And the Braves won another World Series. The season also began a streak of 11 straight years in the playoffs.

The 1957 Milwaukee Braves celebrate a World Series championship! ▶

Tough Days!

Not every season can end with a World Series win. Here are some of the toughest seasons in Braves history:

1911: Playing as the Boston Rustlers, the team couldn't rustle up many wins. They lost a team-record 111 games!

1977: The Braves had one of the league's worst records this year, with 106 losses. It was one of four straight last-place finishes!

1993: The Braves had the best record in baseball, with 104 wins. In the playoffs, though, they were upset by the Phillies. They didn't even get a chance to play in the World Series.

◄ Pitcher Tom Glavine just couldn't watch. His Braves were losing the playoff series to the Phillies in 1993.

Meet the Fans

Atlanta's fans are some of the loudest in baseball! They have enjoyed watching many terrific Braves teams. They got to watch the Braves in the playoffs every year from 1991 through 2005! Braves fans fill Turner Field. They also watch all around America on cable TV.

Turner Field is a great place for Braves fans to watch their favorite team. ▶

Hank Gowdy, Catcher

Heroes Then . . .

No matter where they played, the Braves have always had great players. Hugh Duffy was a great hitter and base runner in the 1890s. Catcher Hank Gowdy helped create the miracle for the 1914 Braves' upset win. In Milwaukee, third baseman Eddie Mathews smacked more than 500 homers. Pitcher Warren Spahn won more than 350 games. Outfielder Hank Aaron was one of the greatest all-around players of all time. Playing in Milwaukee and Atlanta, he had 755 homers, the second-most ever! In the 1980s, outfielder Dale Murphy won two N.L. **Most Valuable Player (MVP)** awards. In the 1990s, pitcher Greg Maddux earned four N.L. **Cy Young Awards** as the top pitcher.

◀ Hank Aaron watches his 714th career homer leave the ballpark in 1973. That tied the record set by the great Babe Ruth.

23

Heroes Now . . .

Today's Braves are a mix of **veteran** stars and young heroes. Third baseman Chipper Jones has been a huge part of the team since 1995. He was the 2008 N.L. batting champ. Derek Lowe only joined the Braves in 2009, but he's now an important pitcher. Catcher Brian McCann is one of the N.L.'s best. Leading them all is **manager** Bobby Cox. He has been in charge of the team since 1990, longer than any other big-league manager.

Jones leads the **offense**, while Lowe stars on the pitching staff. ▶

Chipper Jones, Third Base

Derek Lowe, Pitcher

Brian McCann, Catcher

BAT

BATTING HELMET

BATTING GLOVES

TEAM JERSEY

TEAM JERSEY

TEAM PANTS

CATCHER'S MASK

CATCHER'S MITT

CATCHER'S CHEST PROTECTOR

CATCHER'S SHIN GUARD

BASEBALL CLEATS

Brian McCann, Catcher

Gearing Up

Baseball players all wear a team jersey and pants. They have to wear a team hat in the field and a helmet when batting. Take a look at Chipper Jones and Brian McCann to see some other parts of a baseball player's uniform.

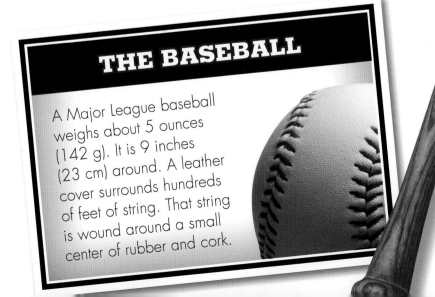

THE BASEBALL

A Major League baseball weighs about 5 ounces (142 g). It is 9 inches (23 cm) around. A leather cover surrounds hundreds of feet of string. That string is wound around a small center of rubber and cork.

SPORTS STATS

Here are some all-time career records for the Atlanta Braves. All the stats are through the 2009 season.

HOME RUNS

Hank Aaron, 733
Eddie Mathews, 493

RUNS BATTED IN

Hank Aaron, 2,202
Chipper Jones, 1,445

BATTING AVERAGE

Billy Hamilton, .338
Hugh Duffy, .332

WINS BY A PITCHER

Warren Spahn, 356

Kid Nichols, 329

STOLEN BASES

Herman Long, 431

Hugh Duffy, 331

WINS BY A MANAGER

Bobby Cox, 2,058

EARNED RUN AVERAGE

Tommy Bond, 2.21

Tom Hughes, 2.22

Glossary

Cy Young Award an award given to the top pitcher in each league

home plate a five-sided rubber pad where batters stand to swing, and where runners touch base to score runs

infield the area around and between the four bases of a baseball diamond

manager the person who is in charge of the team and chooses who will bat and pitch

Most Valuable Player (MVP) a yearly award given to the top player in each league

offense when a team is at bat and is trying to score runs

opponents teams or players that play against each other

outfield the large, grass area beyond the infield of a baseball diamond

veteran a player who has been in a league for several seasons

World Series the Major League Baseball championship, played each year between the winners of the American and National Leagues

Find Out More

BOOKS

Buckley, James Jr. *Eyewitness Baseball*. New York: DK Publishing, 2010.

Stewart, Mark. *Atlanta Braves*. Chicago: Norwood House Press, 2006.

Teitelbaum, Michael. *Baseball*. Ann Arbor, MI: Cherry Lake Publishing, 2009.

Thornley, Stew. *Super Sports Star Chipper Jones*. Berkeley Heights, NJ: Enslow, 2005.

WEB SITES

Visit our Web page for links about the Atlanta Braves and other pro baseball teams.

childsworld.com/links

Note to Parents, Teachers, and Librarians: We routinely verify our Web links to make sure they are safe, active sites—so encourage your readers to check them out!

Index

ABOUT THE AUTHOR

K.C. Kelley has written dozens of books on baseball and other sports for young readers. He has also been a youth baseball coach and called baseball games on the radio. His favorite team? The Boston Red Sox.